QUAIL FARMING FOR BEGINNERS

EVERYTHING YOU NEED TO KNOW

Disclaimer

Copyright © 2015 Francis O. All rights reserved. No part of this publication may be reproduced, stored in a retrieval system, or transmitted in any form or by any means – electronic, mechanical, photocopy, recording, or any other – except for brief quotations in print or online reviews, without the prior permission of the author.

The writing of this material has been a humble undertaking by the author to facilitate anyone interested in quail farming with useful information relevant to subject of the book. While the author has made every effort to ensure that the information contained herein is accurate and up-to-date (at the time of publication), you are encouraged to exercise your own independent skill and judgment when relying on the contents herein. You are encouraged to seek for services of experienced quail / poultry professionals within your area should you be in need of guidance.

This publication is designed to provide competent and reliable information regarding the subject matter covered. However, it is sold with the understanding that the author is not engaged in rendering legal, financial, or other professional advice. The author specially disclaim any liability that is incurred or that which may be incurred from the use of or application of the contents of this book.

Although the author has made every effort to ensure that the information in this book was correct at the time of publication, the author does not assume and hereby disclaim any liability to any party for any loss, damage, or disruption caused by errors or omissions, whether such errors or omissions result from negligence, accident, or any other cause.

Special Dedication

Are you passionate about keeping quail? Are you in search of how best to start quail farming and drive that venture to a sustainable profitable end: for either domestic or commercial gains? If your answer is yes, this book is dedicated to you.

Acknowledgments

I am most appreciative of the many people who offered invaluable views, ideas, and support towards the making of this book.

To Arnold, Steve, Anne, David, Rachael, Moses, Amos, Emmaculate and Dr. Ruth, thank you all, and may the almighty God bless you richly.

Finally, but most important, I thank God for the gift of life, inspiration, knowledge and for His endless blessings upon my life. Indeed, great is His faithfulness. His grace, love and mercy, surely endures forever!

Contents

Two Questions You Must Answer With Clarity Before You Start Raising Quail..**7**

For Starters, What Is Quail?..**11**

Some Quick Facts About Quail......................................**13**

Four Basic Necessities For Effective Raising Of Quail..........**15**

Quail Farming Vs Chicken Farming...............................**20**

How To Start Quail Farming The Right Way....................**25**

Breeding And Reproduction...**30**

How To Select The Right Quail Breed For Raising.............**34**

Feeding Quail...**38**

Other Valuable Tips on Feeding Quail............................**42**

Housing – [Construction, Conditions, and Location]...........**44**

The Most Common Quail Diseases [Causes, Preventions, And Treatments]..**53**

The Most Common Signs Exhibited By Sick Quails............**60**

Factors Making Quails To Be Susceptible to Disease Or Pest Infections **62**

Effective Ways Of Dealing With Quail Pests And Diseases.....**63**

Egg Production, Management, And Incubation..............**66**

The Most Common Causes Of Poor Egg Hatch And Possible Solutions For Each Case..**70**

Products From Quail Farming.....................................**76**

Health/Medicinal Benefits Of Quail Eggs/Meat................**82**

Simple Strategies For Marketing And Selling Quail Products...**86**

How To Profitably Save or Invest Proceeds From Your Quail Farm..**97**

The Five Most Common Quail Farming Mistakes You Should Avoid...**105**

Frequently Asked Questions About Quail Farming............**111**

Two Vital Questions You Must Answer With Clarity Before You Start Raising Quail

"What's my purpose for raising quail? What resources do I have at my disposal?"

Before putting up any quail farming structure, below are the two most vital questions you should ask yourself, and subsequently give clear answers to:

First Question
What's my purpose for raising quail?

Why do you want to raise quail?

- Do you want to raise them just for the fun of it, or as pets in your backyard?

- Or do you want to raise them for family's consumption needs of fresh eggs and nutritious meat?

- Or do you want to raise them for commercial gains?

You must define with clarity your purpose for raising quail. Doing so will help you put effective plans on how best to start and proceed with the whole process.

Second Question
What resources do I have at my disposal?

Some of the basic resources needed to start and run a successful quail farming venture includes: adequate space, right housing, good knowledge on how to care of quail, and how to manage diseases and pests affecting quail. However, significantly, the most vital resource you need is enough amount of money: it does lead towards easy acquisition of all the other necessary quail farming resources. With money, you can acquire adequate space (land), right housing (cages), and also be able to enjoy services of experienced veterinary professionals with world-class knowledge on how to take care of quail.

Why you want to raise quail, coupled with the amount of resources you are willing to put aside will help guide you towards determining the nature and size of your quail farming venture.

For Starters, What Is Quail?

"*According to* **Scripture Alphabet of Animals by Mrs. Harriet N. Cook,** *a quail bird is described to be the size of a pigeon. It is called bird of passage because it does not live in the same place. It spends winter in one country and flies away to another country in spring*"

This chapter is for starters. Those who do not know what a quail bird is, or has never encountered quail bird.

Quail is described as *a kind of game bird within the family of Phasianidae*. It is smaller than a chicken and not as well known as the pigeon (*definition according to vocabulary.com*).

According to *Scripture Alphabet of Animals by Mrs. Harriet N. Cook,* a quail bird is described to be the size of a pigeon. It is called bird of passage because it does not live in the same place. It spends winter in one country and flies away to another country in spring. In their journeys, they fly together in very large flocks, as you have perhaps seen wild geese or pigeons do.

Some quick facts about quail

- Did you know there are more than 120 different quail species around the world? Quail appear small in body size when compared to chickens of same age and sex. Resultantly, they require minimal spaces for housing.

- Quail eggs are cholesterol free. This has made their eggs a favorite for consumption by persons suffering from hypertension. The birds' meat and eggs are preferred alternative sources of protein.

- Quail are resistant to a number of diseases affecting a number of poultry birds. They require minimal to no vaccinations against diseases, if taken good care of.

- On average, mature female quail may start laying eggs at the age of six weeks. They lay an average of 25 eggs in a good month, translating to over 300 eggs in a good year (especially Japanese quails). Thereafter, their rate of egg production may start to decline, depending on quail breed and how they are taken care of.

- Quail chicks are delicate and may seldom survive in very cold or hot weather. Always handle them with extra care and shield them from exposure to extreme weather conditions. And although mature quail can survive in harsh weather conditions, also shield them from exposure to such weather for consistent productivity to be realized.

- From hatching, quail chicks take between 4 to 6 weeks to attain maturity (depending on breed and care given during the rearing period).

- Quails' eggs are multicolored. Several credential research findings shows that that consuming the eggs helps in improving human fertility.

- Some quail breeds are fussy feeders. They may like or dislike the taste, colors, or shapes of certain feeds. Equally, they can sometimes be seen eating for a long time, but they will seldom overeat! They know when to pause and when to stop. Interestingly, they do comfortably feed on commercial chicken feeds.

Four Basic Necessities For Effective Raising Of Quail

"Safe and secure environment, basic knowledge on handling quail pests and diseases, *quality feeds, and* clean, fresh water for drinking*"*

Below are the four basic necessities for effective raising of quail.

1. ## Safe and secure environment

   As you establish an accommodation for your quail, it doesn't have to be a highly elaborate or sophisticated piece of structure. No. What is of utmost importance to the birds is a safe and secure housing, and an environment; where they are free of disturbance and attacks by pests and predators.

   Did you know that many female quails will seldom lay eggs in an insecure environment? And in case they do, the numbers will always be inconsistent and dismal!

2. ## Basic knowledge on handling quail pests and diseases

   You do not necessarily need an in-depth knowledge on all the pests and diseases affecting quail in order to be effective at raising healthy and disease free flock. However, you need to arm yourself with the basics on managing quail pests and diseases should they surface within your flock.

   Some of the best pest and disease management practices you should have basic knowledge on are:

- How to dust the birds, and the birds' accommodation with appropriate pesticides to help keep pests and parasites at bay.

- How to select healthy birds for raising.

- How to identify and quarantine sick-looking birds to help contain spread of any contagious disease within the flock.

- How to de-worm the birds occasionally to help control attack and spread of worms and other internal infestations.

- How to debeak birds with noted pecking disorders.

- And last but not least, you need to have contacts and access to trained and experienced poultry professionals within your area for ease of reach in case of any disease outbreak.

3. Quality feeds

Just like human beings, quail too do require well balanced diet for quality output. For the birds to grow strong, healthy and be able to produce quality meat and eggs, they need quality and well balanced feeds: rich in carbohydrates, proteins, vitamins etc. You must therefore ensure the feeds contain right amounts of nutrients. Avoid feeds with poor nutritional values, and wet or moldy feeds.

Wet and moldy feeds can easily poison the birds. Equally, such feeds can easily act as favorable hiding places for disease causing organisms.

4. Clean, fresh water for drinking

Giving the birds sufficient clean, fresh water for drinking will enable them to produce clean and fresh meat and eggs. The egg-laying birds need water for egg development. Therefore, lack of clean, fresh water may result into lack of egg formation, subsequently hindering their egg-laying ability. It's that simple.

The quality of drinking water you give quail determines the quality of products the birds will hand you. Summarily, the quality of what goes in determines the quality of output. Giving them clean, fresh water will result in production of clean, fresh eggs and meat.

Give them adequate amount of clean, fresh water placed at strategic positions where they do not need any unnecessary strain to access it. Give them the water at room temperature: avoid very cold or very hot waters since they will avoid drinking such.

Quail Farming Vs Chicken Farming

"It is openly evident quail farming appear more lucrative. It's more profitable with less labor and capital intensive, than chicken farming. The benefits of quail farming surpass those of chicken farming in almost all the aspects compared"

Quail Farming

- As already indicated, quail appear smaller in body size when compared with chicken of similar age. Raising them will resultantly require smaller cages (small housing space).

- In terms of feeds, quail do consume an equivalent of one eighth of chicken feeds. And certain breeds are known fussy feeders.

- Most quail breeds are disease resistant. They require less attention and few to no vaccinations/treatments against diseases.

- Quail products; meat and eggs, are richly nutritious. These products have been scientifically proven to contain beneficial health and medicinal values.

- Keeping quail require less capital input, but with good return on investment.

- Did you know quail can be sourced from the wild? Quail are natural wild birds hence do not need to be necessarily reared, especially for meat consumption. You can as well hunt them in the wild or forest.

- Quail can be conveniently transported from one place to

another due to their smaller body size and light weight, as compared to chickens of similar ages which are slightly heavy.

- Quail products; chicks, eggs and meat, fetch higher market prices as compared to similar chicken products.

Chicken Farming

- Compared to quail of similar age, chickens appear bigger in size. As a result, they require bigger spaces for housing.

- Chickens require feeds in large quantities as compared to quails.

- Chickens are prone to infection by a number of poultry-related diseases; hence do require close and constant monitoring plus vaccinations and treatments unlike quail.

- Chickens' meat and eggs are less nutritious, and contain minimal health benefits. Equally, they have minimal to no proven medicinal values when compared to quail eggs and meat.

- Chicken farming is more capital intensive with minimal return on investment than quail farming.

- There are no alternatives to sourcing chickens for raising. They are domestic animals, unlike quail which can be sourced from the wild.

- Chickens are heavy in weight when compared to quail of similar age and sex. It is therefore burdensome transporting a large portion of chickens from one location to another unlike quail.

From the above short comparison, it is openly evident quail farming appear more lucrative. It's more profitable with less labor and capital intensive, than chicken farming. The benefits of quail farming surpass those of chicken farming in almost all the aspects compared.

You can never go wrong out of an investment in quail farming. All you need is good preparation to ensure you start the venture on a right track.

How To Start Quail Farming The Right Way

"In order to maximize returns and reap more profits from quail farming, it is advisable to have a plan. Such plan should clearly capture all the series of events a quail farmer is required to undertake before, during and after starting"

Many people venture into certain kind of businesses due to success stories they have heard or witnessed from people doing similar businesses. Shockingly, many end up being met with frustrations and failures when they roll out such similar ventures on their own. Part of that failure is largely attributed to lack of clear set out goals of that which they intend to achieve.

In order to maximize returns and reap more profits from quail farming, it is advisable to have a plan. Such plan should clearly capture all the series of events a quail farmer is required to undertake before, during and after starting.

The benefits of having the correct quail farming plan prior to starting out can never be overemphasized. It is what will lead a serious quail farmer towards a sustainable and more profitable undertaking.

A good quail farming plan will help a serious quail farmer to determine:

- Purpose for production
- Breeding needs.
- Health needs.
- Feeding needs.
- Housing needs.
- Marketing needs….among others

Having a correct quail farming plan is the first positive step towards starting quail farming on a right track. It is at the core of setting base towards becoming and remaining profitable in the long run.

But with or without the plan, below are some of the basic essentials any quail farmer should have in place in order to engage in a profitable undertaking:

- Get relevant and up-to-date information on raising quail. Summarily, you should know what you are getting into and how best you will profitably stay in it. It's that simple.

- Get the right quail breeds from the start, depending on your purpose for rearing the birds; for domestic gains or for commercial reasons. Always remember that *if you start with undesirable breed, their output will be undesirable too, but if you start with a desirable breed, then their output will be desirable.* It's like the proverbial, 'what you sow is what you reap'

- Have in place a good housing facility, secure space for raising the quails, depending on your purpose for rearing the birds.

- Be armed with correct information on quail feeds and quail disease management. If you feel disadvantaged with such information or knowledge, it is advisable to seek for services of experienced quail or poultry professionals.

- Be armed with the latest relevant information on quail farming industry plus market trends. Go the extra mile and gather similar information on poultry farming as a whole.

There can never be enough information on better ways of starting quail farming and subsequent management of quail farms. Day in day out, new information and technologies emerge that may help improve on the quality of production. It would be of great benefit to look out for such vital information, which would suit your quail farming need. Read relevant materials on quail from newspapers, magazines, journals, books, websites, blogs etc.

Breeding & Reproduction

"Quail thrive well as a group"

Below are some vital points to take into consideration in regard to breeding and reproduction of quail.

- Quail are flock birds (they thrive well as a group). Keep them in a ratio of one male to two females, or one male to three females (these are the most recommended ratio if you intend to get fertilized eggs from the layers).

- Identify and quickly isolate any bird with noted pecking disorder. If possible, debeak such birds. The tendency to peck other birds is commonly exhibited by most male birds. If not checked, they can end up making their victims go blind, and in extreme cases, even end up causing deaths of their victims.

- It is advisable to stick to one type of quail breed. Avoid mixing different breeds as they may not be friendly to one another (they may not get along).

- Quail start laying eggs when they attain 6 weeks old. They then progress to 70% of egg production on the 8th week. Therefore, as they approach egg laying week, you should pair one male to two females, or one male to utmost three females. (If you intend to get fertilized eggs from them).

- Quail take an average of 16-18 days to successfully incubate their eggs. When the chicks are hatched, they usually have an attachment of egg yolk in their lower body (abdomen). Do not scrap this yolk away since they need it as a source of food for the first few days (two days), as they get acclimatized to a new way of life.

- In case you buy quail chicks elsewhere, feed them on electrolytes and some slightly warm water mixed with vitamins. Additionally, give them clean, fresh water.

- Do not be scared at the size of quail chicks. Some may appear usually tiny, but note that they have the ability to feed on their own. However, the chicks are delicate and sensitive to cold and hot temperatures. You should therefore, ensure you shield them from exposure to such temperatures.

- To prevent quail chicks from drowning in water troughs, use small-sized troughs, and you should also half-fill the water troughs with glass or stone marbles.

Note

Sometimes quail, especially, mature males of certain breeds, have a tendency of making noise (some soft sound). This should not scare you. Instead, it should guide you towards positioning quail house in a location where such noise would not interfere with your peace, or your neighbor's.

How To Select The Right Quail Breed For Raising

"In Quail farming, the input determines the output. The type of quail breed you start out with will play a huge role in determining the quality of gains from your venture"

In Quail farming, the input determines the output. The type of quail breed you start out with will play a huge role in determining the quality of gains from your venture. Therefore, you need to be keen when selecting your initial flock.

The following five tips should help guide you when getting your initial flock.

- Visit at least three different local quail farmers to see the quail breeds they are keeping, their purpose of raising the birds, and the production capabilities of those breeds.

- Are there licensed and reputable quail breeders or quail dealer outlets within your region? These are the people/places you should give first preference when you decide to buy your first flock. Aim to acquire the best performing breeds available from them.

- Avoid purchase of breeding flock with deformities. They may not be productive for a desirable period of time.

- At the start, stick to one type of quail breed. Avoid mixing different breeds as they may not be friendly to one another, especially if they are being raised in the same cages.

- Equally, avoid purchase of flock of different sizes, and those of different colors. They may most probably not get along (they will always want to pick a fight), resulting into low, unprofitable outputs.

- Establish mortality history or diseases history of the breed you intend to purchase. Most breeders or dealers have these records in their possessions.

- If you decide to purchase quail eggs for incubation, insist on getting eggs with equal (similar) sizes, shapes and colors. Equally, get eggs with no abnormalities.

Feeding Quail

"Quail need right feeds in right quantities to help them stay active and productive as they grow"

For your quail farming to remain a profitable venture, the birds must be well-fed on nutritious and well balanced feeds. The correct amount of feeding will allow the birds to give satisfactory output.

Due to their small body sizes, quail are adapted to consuming fewer amounts of feeds. Interestingly, they usually eat as much as they should. You should therefore never worry about any risk of overfeeding them. They know when to stop.

Quail need right feeds in right quantities to help them stay active and productive as they grow. Well balanced feeds assist their bodies to grow strong and develop immunity against possible attack poultry related diseases.

In case you buy quail chicks from a breeder or a quail farmer who doesn't take good care of the birds, ensure you feed the chicks on electrolytes and some warm water mixed with vitamins.

Below is a simple guide on feeding quail; from chicks to adult quail.

Starter Feeds

Immediately the chicks are hatched, start them off with chick starter. Chick starters are usually rich in proteins which the chicks are in dire need of at that development stage.

Feed them on the starter feeds until they are 3-4 weeks old.

The protein content within the starter feeds usually varies. Notably, starter feeds for layers normally has higher levels of protein than the starter feeds for males.

As a good recommendation, you can feed them on game bird feeds /turkey feeds (a starter feed with an average protein content of 25%). However, at the start, you need to liaise with nearby trained and experienced quail farmers/breeders or poultry vets for recommendations on the best starter feeds that will best suit your quail breed.

Regular Feeds

Graduate the starter feeds to regular feeds when the birds attain 4 weeks. Put them on the starter feeds at between 4-6 weeks.

There are different regular feeds, or what others refer to as growers mash, for male quails (broilers) and for female quails (hens).

Ensure you get a good recommendation for the right growers mash from experienced quail bird farmers /breeders/ poultry vets (the names of these feeds differ from one country to another).

Take note that even at that stage, the starter feeds should still be constituted with a good percentage of proteins.

Other Valuable Tips on Feeding Quail

Did you know that quail can comfortably consume commercial chicken feeds? However, you should increase the protein content of commercial chicken feeds to be compatible with the high protein levels required by quail.

Since quail are known fussy eaters, you should buy quail feed pellets in mini sacks of say 25kgs each (in case you are keeping a few pairs of quails), as the feeds may go off before your quail feed on all of it

Non-medicated game bird feed is invaluably ideal to give to the birds as it rich in protein.

In the absence of commercial quail feed, the birds can be fed on soya meals, groundnut cakes, fish meals, sorghum, sunflower cakes, maize seeds (corn seeds), deoiled rice bran etc.

In addition to provision of quality feeds, do not forget to give the birds clean and fresh water for drinking. Equally, give them grit to help them improve on food digestion.

You can supplement their diet with kitchen scraps such as sweet corn, grated carrot, and broccoli, chunks of apple, lettuce, cut cabbages and even peas. You can also feed them on millet or mealworms.

Notably, mature males tend to shy off from eating mealworms. Instead, they present the mealworms to the hens as a sign of appreciation.

Note

The more you feed quail on different feeds, the more you will learn about their favorite feeds.

Avoid feeding quail fresh cuttings from the garden as it is easy to mix in a poisonous plant. Equally, don't give them avocado or chocolate since the two are poisonous to a number of birds.

Housing
[Construction, Conditions, And Location]

"One of the many advantages of keeping quail is the relatively small-spaced houses they require for accommodation as compared to the slightly large-spaced houses required by chickens of same ages"

One of the many advantages of keeping quail is the relatively small-spaced houses they require for accommodation as compared to the slightly large-spaced houses required by chickens of same ages. Summarily, you'll always end up spending less on quail accommodation as compared to chickens'.

The type accommodation that you need to use for your quail is largely dependent on your purpose for keeping them. Raising the birds for commercial gains require use of bigger houses and more space, while keeping them for domestic ends do require small space.

Below are some of the most important basics that you must put into consideration when constructing and locating quail accommodation.

- Security and comfortability of quail
- Efficiency in the management quail
- Convenience to quail farmer

a) Security and comfortability of quail

Quail tend to be unproductive in an insecure housing and in an insecure location. Their house should therefore be well constructed to effectively shield the birds from strong winds, hot sun, rodents like snakes, and other domestic animals like cats and dogs.

When constructing quail cages, the most recommended guideline is to allocate between (2–2.5)sq ft square feet for every adult bird. And the bottom half (or ¾ of the bottom of cages) should be made with strong materials.

You can extend a wire mesh a foot from the cage's bottom to help in baring rodents and domestic animals like cats and dogs.

b) Efficiency in the management of quail

Since you should be undertaking timely cleaning of quail house, it is advisable to position the house at a convenient place, where you can have quick and easy access to it at any given time of the day or night. (more read below under 'Locating Quail House'– *Proximity to the main house*).

Efficiency in the management of the birds should be characterized by clean cages, clean feeders and waterers, adequate feeds placed at dry, strategic and secure points, and healthy flock free of infection by diseases and parasites.

The bottom of the cages should have removable plates (preferably wooden), to aid in clearing of the birds' droppings.

When you construct larger cages, each unit should be approximately 6.5 feet in length, and 1.5 foot in width, and partitioned into between 5 - 6 subunits (depending on your choice). You can opt to arrange the cages in tiers above to save on space.

c) Convenience to quail farmer

Equipments inside the house should be fittingly arranged to avail to the farmer enough space to carry out day-to-day maintenance works.

The design of the house should not be too complex. If it's complex, then it might hinder the farmer from carrying out timely cleaning and dusting of the birds against pests.

Housing Conditions

Under housing conditions, let's quickly examine the three most vital conditions necessary inside any standard quail house.

1. Temperature

Quail thrive best under temperatures of between 40°F to 65°F or 70°F. Ensure their accommodation has correct temperature at any given time of the day or night.

During night, the birds need warm temperature since they are generally inactive. However, during daytime, they can handle both warm and cold temperatures, since they are active (but this depends on breed and age of the birds).

Mature quail tend to adapt easily with temperature change unlike their chicks.

Construct the house with cold insulators to keep it warm during winter. Equally, provide enough ventilation to cool down the house during hot summers. Extreme temperatures: either very cold or very hot, may stress the birds and make them uncomfortable, resulting into dismal productivity.

2 Ventilations

A properly ventilated quail house will provide the birds with fresh air and sweep away any unnecessary moisture off the house. In most instances, proper ventilations aid in drying up the birds' droppings, thus reducing exposure of the birds to some common diseases like Coccidiosis.

Aim to keep the quails' house in a dry state to curb any emergence and thriving of disease causing germs. Equally, some of the most common quail diseases like pneumonia and cold-related infection will not easily affect the birds in such dry environments.

Replace with speed any leaking space on roofs to bar the unnecessary dripping of contaminated water which may eventually mix in with feeds, possibly turning the feeds into poisonous mold. In equal measure, quickly replace leaking water troughs and feed containers.

3 Light

The egg production levels of quail are influenced by the amount of light that they are exposed to. Ensure that their house has access to light (natural or artificial), for an extended period (not less than 13 or 14 hours in a day). Exposure to right amount of light is vital when the birds begin laying eggs.

Quail need more of light and less of darkness. Find creative ways of exposing their accommodation to natural light (sunlight), especially during morning hours. They need sunlight for vitamin D. The sun also aids in drying up any moist surfaces which may harbor disease-causing germs. In instances where sunlight may be inadequate, use of artificial light is highly encouraged.

Note

One ideal way to help you decide on the type of housing unit you may require for the birds is by visiting at least two quail farms within your region. From those farms, you'll have a rough idea, or possibly end up settling on a befitting housing design to adopt.

Some of the materials commonly used in the construction quail houses are: iron sheets, timber, plywood, 1/4 inch wire mesh and nails of different sizes (depending on the various types and sizes of timber you intend to use in building the frameworks of the cages).

A good guideline is to allocate between (2 to 2.5) sq ft square feet for every adult bird. However, before then, if you have quail chicks, you can raise them on a floor with five to six of them fitting a square feet on floor. They can then be transferred to cages after four weeks.

If you are raising the birds for commercial egg production, they can be housed in colonies of 8 to 10 birds per cage. However, for breeding purposes, the male birds should be paired with females in the ratio of 1 male to 2 females, or 1 male to three females.

Locating Quail House

When it comes to identification of the most ideal place for locating/putting up quail house, you should keenly pay attention to the below factors.

- Drainage

    It's advisable to place quail house in a slightly sloppy setup. This is essential towards enabling easy drainage of any unwanted water beneath the accommodation.

- Proximity to the main house

    Quails' droppings often emit foul smell, especially when exposed to warm temperature or sunlight. This would make positioning of their house close to the main house appear unsanitary. On the other hand, a closer balancing act is needed on this aspect. You will always need to have a fast and easy access to the birds' house at any given time of the day or night.

    The birds' house should not be far away from the main house as you will need to make timely trips to: collect eggs, replenish both drinking waters and feeds, and to attend to the birds.

- Exposure to adequate hours of light

    Various researches show that presence of sunlight makes a number of birds happy. That's why you may wake up to hear most birds excitedly making noise at sunrise. Quails too love light and best thrive under well lit houses.

    Quail are generally active in the morning hours, when exposed to light. Wherever you settle on locating the birds' house, ensure it's sufficiently exposed to enough natural light, sunlight. And in the absence of natural light, ensure the house enjoys sufficient artificial lighting.

The Most Common Quail Diseases
(Causes, Preventions, and Treatments)

"Quail are hardy birds known to be resistant to a number of diseases affecting most poultry birds"

An average quail farmer may not clearly identify and offer an effective diagnosis and treatments to quail diseases at the farm level without relevant training, experience and equipment. Specifically, without training and proper equipment, it would be difficult to diagnose internal infections.

Quail are hardy birds known to be resistant to a number of diseases affecting most poultry birds. Interestingly, lots of research on diseases affecting quail is ongoing and hopefully, future quail farmers will have a broader knowledge on dealing with the most common and emerging quail diseases.

Below are the four most common quail diseases, preventions, and treatments.

1. Coccidiosis

Coccidiosis is a parasitic infection which has a severe effect on the digestive tracts of infected quail birds. It normally attacks quail which are less than 7 weeks old. (Birds beyond 7 weeks of age are usually resistant to coccidiosis, but in cases of attack, the impact is usually not as severe as it is to birds below 7 weeks of age).

Since coccidiosis affects the digestive tracts of the birds, the infected birds would generally slow down and eventually stop eating. They will subsequently grow weak, pale and weak legged. If not attended to on time, the infected birds may die.

Prevention and treatment

Coccidiosis affects quail and other poultry birds out of poor management of farms i.e. failure to keep the poultry houses clean and dry. Coccidiosis thrives where there is a buildup of wet quail droppings and in moist areas around water points and feeders.
You therefore need to ensure the cages are dry and free of wet quail droppings. It's advisable constructing the areas around feeders and water points using wire mesh. This ensures no quail dropping accumulates within the cages.

Certain quail feeds are laced with coccidiostat; a drug that helps prevents infection by coccidiosis. To the birds which are not yet infected with coccidiosis, the consumption of coccidiostat in the feeds allows them limited infection with coccidiosis, and thereafter, they develop immunity against the disease. Also, consult an experienced poultry vet for recommendation of the best anticoccidial to use to contain coccidiosis.

2. Capillary Worms/Thread Worms/Crop Worms)

The second disease or rather parasite affecting quail is worms. Specifically, the most dangerous of the worms are those that infect the lining of the birds' crops. Capillary worms, scientifically known as *Capillaria spp.* falls in this category.

The infection caused by capillary worms can never be diagnosed by merely looking at the bird physically. It's only when the crop of an infected bird is removed, or when the crop of a bird which has died of the infection is removed and opened, then worms which appear thread-like can be seen lining across the tissue fragments of the bird's crop.

The infected birds often eat a lot, but always appear as if starving. And in the last stages of infection, the infected birds may experience difficulty in breathing, and defecations of infected birds may have accompaniments of worms. These are the three most common physical symptoms of a bird infected with capillary worms.

Prevention and treatment

Capillary worms usually thrive in wet droppings and in wet areas around feeders and waterers. The best way to control infection and spread of capillary worms is by constructing the base of the birds' cages with wire mesh.

Spaces on the wire mesh would not allow build-up of quail' wet droppings and thus, will prevent the birds from picking the disease from the cages, and lessen its spread, if any. The cages too should be raised from the ground.

To treat capillary worms, it is recommended you use a correct wormer (de-wormer). Consult an experienced poultry vet within your area for recommendation on an appropriate wormer (de-wormer), since the names of these drugs differ from one country to another.

3. Histomoniasis

This is one of the most lethal diseases affecting quail. Histomoniasis, also known as a blackhead, is a protozoan infection which attacks a number of poultry breeds. In fact, it is usually referred to as a disease of the larger fowl unit.

Histomoniasis infects the liver of quail and immediately, starts to produce necrotic lesions which eventually results into fatal liver damages of the infected birds. The infected birds often exhibit restlessness, poor appetite, loss of feathers, and sulfur-like colored droppings.

Prevention and treatment

It is believed chickens which have recovered from histomoniasis are its carrier. Therefore, as a precautionary measure, avoid mixing chickens with quail birds under the same housing.

For treatment purposes, use relevant wormers (de-wormers), to help eliminate cecal worms which transmit histomoniasis. However, the most effective treatment for histomoniasis lies in its prevention.

4. Ulcerative Enteritis

Ulcerative enteritis is another destructive quail disease. From its name, the disease occurs like an ulcer on the internal linings of the infected birds' intestines. However, the most effective way to diagnose Ulcerative enteritis is through laboratory analysis.

The disease can easily be transmitted from one infected bird to another through contact with the droppings of the infected bird. It has too been established that birds which have recovered from ulcerative enteritis are usually its carrier.

Prevention and treatment

The most effective ways to prevent spread of this fatal disease lies in exercising clean sanitary measures and in the quick identification and quarantine of the infected birds.

Clean up the cages off any wet droppings, and it is essential the holding areas of the cages be built with wire mesh to help stop any accumulation of the birds' wet droppings.

For treatment, liaise with an experienced poultry vet for recommendations on effective drugs to use.

Note

Before administering any diseases control, it's vital to first consult a veterinary practitioner for guidance.

The Most Common Signs Exhibited By Sick Quails

Just like most poultry birds, sick quails may tend to exhibit some of the below characteristics:

- Numb, un-alert and unresponsive

    Sick quails may appear numb and un-alert. They may appear unresponsive to any form of touch, and will mostly be seen bored or sleeping within their accommodation. If standing, they will tend to exhibit an abnormal posture.

- Decline in egg production

    If there is a sudden drop in the number of eggs laid by the hens, that could a possible sign of disease infection within the flock.

- Extreme body temperatures

    You should occasionally check the body temperatures of the birds to establish if any could be exhibiting unusually high or unusually low temperature as such could be a sign of sickness.

- Lack of appetite

    Sick quails lack normal appetite and will resort to consuming reduced quantity of feeds.

- Lackluster behavior

    Sick quails may appear gloomy, and are largely uninterested even when you give them feeds or water.

- Observable defects in defecations

    When the defecation appears bloodstained, that could be a sure sign of internal infection. If it has an accompaniment of worms or larvae, that's a sign of possible parasitic infection. If it is hard, or watery, those could be signs of possible dehydration and diarrhea respectively.

- Difficulty in breathing

    Blocked mucus membranes, or any observable or hearable sound suggesting difficulty in breathing by bird could be a sign of respiratory infection, possibly pneumonia.

- Rough or loose plumage

    If the feathers are falling off, or appear rough in texture, be sure to check the bird closely for any possible disease or parasite infection.

Note

When you spot a bird exhibiting signs of sickness, isolate it from the rest of the flock, as fast as you possibly can. Afterwards, seek for the services of a trained and experienced poultry vet to help you diagnose and possibly treat the affected bird. Do not try to offer any form of treatment to a sick quail on your own if you aren't sure about the disease it might be suffering from. Things may turn tragic!

Factors Making Quails To Be Susceptible To Disease Or Pest Infections

Below are some of the leading factors making quails to be susceptible to disease or pest infections.

- **Age**

    Did you know that older quail are usually prone to disease infections? This is due to their weakened body defense mechanisms. Equally, younger quails too are prone to infection by certain diseases due to their not-fully developed body immune system.

- **Physical injuries**

    Any physical injury inflicted on any part of a quail's body may make such wound susceptible to bacterial infection. Such injuries may be inflicted by other quail, quail owner, or even by the affected quail itself.

- **Environment**

    Very cold or very chilly weather conditions may make it possible for quail to contract respiratory diseases like pneumonia.

- Sex of quail

    Did you know that due to their frequencies in laying eggs, the egg laying birds are more delicate and more prone to disease infections as compared to roosters?

- Poor sanitation

    Unhygienic housing conditions may easily spur outbreak of certain contagious diseases like Coccidiosis.

- Mixing of other poultry breeds with quails

    This too may easily facilitate spread of contagious diseases within your flock. If say you mix quail and chickens in the same housing, any chicken suffering from a disease like histomoniasis may easily transmit it to quail.

Effective Ways Of Dealing With Quail Pests And Diseases

Below are some of the effective ways to help you deal with the pests and diseases affecting quail

- Always raise the birds under sanitary conditions. The moment you choose to raise your birds negligently, under unsanitary conditions, be rest assured that when they fall sick and the best of drugs are administered, such drugs may be rendered ineffective. Raising quail under sanitary conditions is therefore your first step towards keeping healthy birds.

- Ensure the birds' house is always clean and properly disinfected. Wet and uncollected quails' droppings around water points and feeding zones may expose the birds to some deadly infections like Coccidiosis.

- Exercise timely dusting of the birds with appropriate pesticides to help keep external parasites away.

- Quail house should be well constructed to shield the birds from wind, hot sun, rodents like snakes, and other domestic pets like cats and dogs.

- Construct their house with cold insulators to keep the house warm during winter, and provide enough ventilation to cool down the house during hot summer. Equally, the house should have adequate exposure to light (natural or artificial).

- Always feed your flock on quality and well balanced diet. Purchase quail feeds and other feed containing the right amounts of nutrients needed by the birds. If done right, you should expect quality eggs and meat from your flock, coupled with hardy birds resistant to many diseases.

- Give the birds clean, fresh water for drinking, placed at strategic positions where they do not need any unnecessary strain to access to it. It is usually advisable to give them water at room temperature. Avoid giving them very cold or very hot water as they will avoid drinking such.

- The moment some quail begin to appear physically weak or gloomy, isolate them from the rest of the flock, as fast as you possibly can, and have them closely examined for any possible illness.

- De-worm the birds regularly using recommended de-wormers. This will aid in preventing infestations by worms and other protozoan diseases.

- De-beak any noted cannibal with the flock to bar them from inflicting wounds on other birds, which may subsequently make the wounded birds be susceptible to bacterial infections, or death.

Egg Production, Management, And Incubation

"With good care, quail lay an average of 26 eggs in a good month, translating to more than 300 eggs in a good year"

Egg production

Depending on the type of quail breed and care given, mature female quail usually start laying multicolored or white small oval-sized eggs at between the ages of 6 to 8 weeks.

With good care, quail lay an average of 26 eggs in a good month, translating to more than 300 eggs in a good year (like the Japanese quail). Thereafter, their rate of egg production may start to decline, although the rate of decline would highly depend on care given.

If you take good care of them through provision of quality feeds, clean drinking water, and a secure accommodation, then they may consistently continue laying a good number of eggs, for an extended period of time.

When female quail reach egg-laying period, give them enough quality feeds, feed supplements, clean water for drinking, and adequate exposure to light. As already pointed out, they will tend to lay eggs consistently when they are exposed to enough amount of light.

Management

Regularly collect the eggs, at least twice a day. Once collected, the eggs should be stored with pointed ends facing downwards, in a humid environment.

Before you put the eggs in an incubator, ensure they are first stored at room temperature.

Do not attempt to wash any dirty egg with water. Doing so may block the natural egg protective layers and expose the washed eggs to entry by organisms.

Do not hold the eggs for longer than 8 days in the storage facility. Doing so may greatly hinder their hatchability.

Incubation

One of the main causes of poor egg hatch lies in incorrect management of egg incubator. Poor control of temperatures and humidity inside the incubator can turn out to be disastrous to egg hatching.

Ensure the incubator has the right and consistent temperatures and humidity throughout the incubation period. Have the incubator placed inside a room where no change in temperature and humidity can easily occur.

Unclean and poorly disinfected incubator or hatcher may too contribute to poor egg hatch. Therefore, ensure the incubator is properly cleaned and disinfected before use.

The Most Common Causes of Poor Egg Hatch And Possible Solutions For Each Case

"However long you leave infertile eggs in a properly functioning incubator, they will never hatch!"

It is every quail farmers' dream to see all incubated eggs successfully hatch into chicks, ready for the next phase; raising, selling to clients, etc. However, there are several instances in which incubated quail eggs usually fail to hatch.

Below are some of the common causes of poor egg hatch, and possible solutions for each case:

- ## Incubating infertile eggs

    However long you leave infertile eggs in a properly functioning incubator, they will never hatch! Infertile eggs are usually a result of lack of mating between male and female quail prior to egg formation.

    What causes lack of mating may include: disturbance of the birds during mating time, raising of crippled or deformed male quail, keeping too many female quail around a single male.

    ### Solution

    To help curb this, you should candle the eggs before and during incubation (before the 15th day), to help detect any infertile egg.

    But before then, you should correctly pair the males and the females in the correct ratio (one male to two females, or one male to three females) to help guarantee high chances of fertility of the laid eggs.

And last but not least, keep the birds away from disturbance, and desist from using deformed or crippled males for mating during the egg laying period.

- # Poor egg handling and storage prior to incubation

    These two are other common reasons why most eggs never hatch, however long they are presented for incubation.

    Poor egg handling practices include washing of dirty eggs with water, touching the eggs with dirty hands, and putting the eggs in the storage facility with some force - possibly cracking them in the process.

    Equally, holding the eggs for a longer duration in the storage facility may contribute to their poor hatchability.

    ## Solution

    Ensure the eggs are properly handled with care during storage (prior to incubation) to help minimize their chances of cracking. Equally, do not hold the eggs for longer than ten days in the storage room, prior to presenting them for incubation.

- **Incubating eggs from older breeds of quails**

    Female quail aged three years and above would most probably lay infertile eggs. Notably, the eggs from such birds may appear fertile when candled, but still end up failing to hatch when incubated.

    ### Solution

    Always incubate fertilized eggs from younger but mature breeds of quail.

- **Poor egg incubation practices**

    The two most common poor egg incubation practices are: failure to turn the eggs during incubation, and lack of favorable conditions inside an incubator.

    The main reason for turning the eggs during incubation is to guarantee uniform heating of the incubated eggs. Failure to do so may result into overheating of one side of the eggs, thus making them unfit to hatch.

    Equally, remember that for a fertile quail egg to hatch, the incubator has to provide: suitable temperature, relative humidity, and adequate amount of fresh air to the incubated egg. Poor control of temperatures and humidity inside the incubator can hinder egg hatching.

    ### Solution

During incubation, commit to turning the eggs at least three times each twenty four hours (if using manual incubator). However, you can use an automatic egg incubator with the ability to turn the eggs at 180^0, three times each 24 hours.

Always use properly functioning egg incubators with proven ability to hatch quail eggs. If unsure about the right functioning of any incubator, simply avoid using it.

And if you reside in an area which experiences rapid power failure, have a power back up installed for the incubator (to cushion the incubated eggs against sudden changes in temperatures).

- **Poor sanitation**

    Generally, poor sanitation contributes to laying of unclean eggs by the birds. And chances of such unclean eggs being hatched are usually minimal.

    Equally, unclean and poorly disinfected incubators or hatchers may make significant contribution to poor egg hatch.

    ### Solution

    Always raise the birds in the most hygienic setup possible. Their accommodation, feeders and drinkers should be properly cleaned and rightly disinfected. The incubator too should be clean and appropriately disinfected.

Products From Quail Farming

"You can't profitably go wrong in quail farming if you specifically focus on your area of interest, and put in your best foot forward"

To profitably raise quail, you must know what products to expect from the birds, and make necessary plans to maximize on their production. You can't profitably go wrong in quail farming if you specifically focus on your area of interest, and put in your best foot forward.

Below are some of the products and by products from quail farming. The decision on which products you want to settle on producing at your farm is your personal call to make.

- **Infertile eggs**

    When you raise female quail in isolation from male quail, they will lay infertile eggs, once they reach egg-laying age. It is the absence of mating between mature male and mature female quail which result into the laying of infertile eggs by the layers.

    The infertile eggs are mostly common within the setups of commercial quail farming. You will find a number of these eggs being sold in groceries, supermarkets, and food outlets. These eggs are consumed daily by the masses across the globe since they can never hatch chicks.

    It is estimated that one quail egg contains nutritional value equivalent to four times that which is found in a chicken's egg. These eggs are popularly referred to as "wonder eggs"; they have been proven to contain enormous health and medicinal benefits.

- ## Fertilized eggs

    When you raise female quail in good proportion to male quails, they will lay fertilized eggs. Fertilized eggs are a result of mating between mature male and mature female quail.

    Fertilized eggs have the potential of hatching chicks. They are mostly suitable for incubation, or for selling to those in need of them.

    In order to guarantee fertility of quail eggs, it is advisable; as already stated, to pair one male quail with two females, or utmost three females to one male. That's the recommended pairing ratio which may yield fertile quail eggs: any ratio beyond that is not guaranteed to produce fertilized eggs.

- ## Quail chicks

    After successful completion of incubation period, fertilized eggs are expected to hatch into chicks. A few days' old chicks are the most preferred age to acquire and start raising quail.

    At the point of purchasing the chicks, you should look out for good breeds with proven potential. If you start your flock with undesirable breed, then you may get frustrated throughout your quail farming venture!

From hatching, the chicks should be well taken care of: with provision of the right feeds, clean water, and timely medications, to ensure they grow healthy and become productive when they come of age.

- **Point of lay birds**

    These are quail between the ages of 5-6 weeks, and are at the stage, or approaching that stage of laying eggs. Once acquired, they will immediately begin laying eggs.

    From hatching, the birds should be well fed on right compositions of feeds to ensure they attain maturity at the right age, and start laying eggs at the right time.

- **Manure**

    Quails' wastes are useful by-products for farming purposes. The birds' droppings are organic in nature, with high levels of nitrogen. They are therefore, highly beneficial to a number of agricultural plants.

- **Meat**

    You can opt to raise broilers, specifically for meat production, or have a mix up of layers and broilers. Notably, when layers cease to lay eggs, they become 'available' to be slaughtered for their meat.

    Quail meat can be prepared into various delicacies as per one's preference. It can also be packed into frozen form to be supplied to supermarkets and restaurants. Equally, you can smoke quail meat on special orders. It is delicious and can stay preserved for a long period of time.

Health/Medicinal Benefits Of Quail Eggs/Meat

"It is with no doubt that quail eggs have a delicious taste. Their nutritional value has equally been proven to be higher than those found in chickens"

More than eight years ago, some researchers established that quail eggs contain 13% of proteins, while chicken eggs have around 10% of proteins. They also established that quail eggs contain around 139μg of vitamin B1, compared with 55μg found in chickens' eggs. They further established that the birds' eggs have low cholesterol levels and are rich in choline, which is a chemical, required by the human brain for better functioning.

It is with no doubt that quail eggs have a delicious taste. Their nutritional value has equally been proven to be higher than those found in chickens.

A lot has been covered by several researchers, authors, and different media outlets across the globe about the potential of quail eggs being able to fight and possibly cure diseases such as *Arthritis, Asthma, Anemia, Heart diseases, Digestive track disorders, Ulcers, and Gastritis.*

Equally, the "wonder eggs" have been reported to have the potential to:
- ✓ Remove toxins and heavy metals from the blood
- ✓ Posses a strong anti-cancer effects and may help thwart cancerous growth and nourish the prostate gland and restore sexual potency in men.
- ✓ Enhance good memory and brain activity growth
- ✓ Suitable for good looking and healthy skin.

On the other hand, the bird's meat is a delicious white meat with extremely low skin fat, hence low cholesterol level. It is one of the best alternative sources of white meat. Equally, the meat is highly rich in micronutrients with a range of vitamins like vitamin B complex, Vitamin E, Vitamin K and Folic Acid.

A number of today's nutritionists would readily recommend the consumption of quail meat to persons with high levels of cholesterol.

Simple Strategies For Marketing And Selling Quail Products

"the greatest secret to finding a lucrative market for quail products is for any serious quail farmer to venture out and create a market of their own"

It takes time, discipline and patience to extract any gainful returns out of an investment in any business venture.

The main challenge faced by a majority of quail farmers is the crazy idea of trying to sell all their products in the same market, using similar sales and marketing strategies. In the end, pricing eventually becomes a major issue; the lower the price, the higher the chances of making a sale.

Shockingly, even making that sale becomes a matter of probability. It's never guaranteed!

Let's play a scenario where in a given area, all quail farmers are just focusing on one market, say a specific supermarket, to have their products sold there. What would happen in the long run? Eventually, there would be an oversupply of quail products in that supermarket, at unrealistically low prices (every one of them would be scrambling to make a sale). This would finally lead to desperate sales acts by a number of the farmers, eventually leading to deaths of their dreams.

So many would be successful quail farmers have given up on the venture simply because of what they perceive as lack of lucrative markets.

Truth is, the greatest secret to finding a lucrative market for quail products is for any serious quail farmer to venture out and create a market of their own. But how?

Below are effective markets and marketing strategies any quail farmer can employ in order to yield profitable returns.

Join Quail Farming or Poultry Farming Groups

There are lots of quail farming groups that are on various social media platforms such as Facebook linked in, twitter, blogs, websites etc. Start out by joining quail farming groups around your region (country). Thereafter, you can join the International ones.

Through such social forums, a quail farmer has an invaluable opportunity to meet fellow farmers who may either be looking for quail products, or may simply want to share/exchange/compare their vital quail farming experiences.

Through joining such groups, a quail farmer has unlimited room to learn more about quail farming from other's experiences. Such groups provide vital forums for soliciting firsthand experiences of other experienced farmers, as they freely share or compare their experiences, and or ask questions.

Joining such groups has provided avenues for most quail farmers to make that very important first sale. And it is in the making of that initial sale that any quail farmer would get the motivation to make relevant adjustments towards more sales in the future.

Export Markets

Finding a viable export market is every quail farmer's nightmare. Almost every commercial quail farmer I have interacted with has this strong desire to export their products in exchange for the lucrative foreign currencies. However, most of them dream of exporting larger quantities that they do not even produce in the first place.

Most quail farmers cannot reliably satisfy the demand of quails products within their regions of operations. The untapped markets and potentials within their countries are still green, and until they are able to fully satisfy local demand, they should never shift their focus to want to export the products to other countries.

China has for a long time been a major export destination for quail products. This has been due to the broad and unique Chinese cuisine, the country's high population, and unending innovative ways of utilizing quail products in several industries. However, the main question is, how can anyone identify specific institutions, individuals or companies in need of importing quail products?

We live in interesting times where any information is now almost freely available over the internet. These are no periods of compiling a specific list of companies dealing in certain specific products and keeping it safe somewhere. From my personal experience, the best way to identify a viable export market is via use of internet. Why would I advocate for use of internet? It's because, most institutions today have an online presence. Therefore, it is easy to identify and locate specific companies, institutions and serious business people that may be in need of quail products via the internet.

All you need is some little time to search for information on any quail product you intend to export, and in flash, all the relevant answers will pop out for you to decide.

I honestly believe that use of internet is an effective and relevant way to locate viable export markets for quail products. Theoretically, this may sound unfulfilling, but practically, it is worth trying.

Note: However, when using internet, take note not to fall into the wrong hands of online fraudsters. Always find ways of verifying the authenticity of your export target before officially engaging them.

Engage Services of Sales/Marketing Professional

If you have doubts in your sales and marketing capabilities, or want help in making a good number of sales, you can simply employ services of someone else; a professional in sales and marketing.

However, take note to only engage services of such persons if you have adequate stock or adequate supply of quail products. Equally, you should have adequate finances to compensate the person, based on contract agreement. Out of personal experience, the best way to engage any sales professional is though working on an agreement on certain targets. In fact, there is a popular sales rule that *figures don't lie*. Let the figures delivered by the sales person determine how much he/she should take home.

Target Local Supermarkets

Selling quail products to local supermarkets is every quail farmer's dream idea. This is because of the many customers who shop in such places. It is therefore, a guarantee that any product stocked in any supermarket has to be seen by clients, and may possibly be bought at the end of the day.

Truth is, supermarkets can be lucrative venues for selling quail products, if and only if fewer farmers make available their quail related products there. However, if many farmers avail their products for sale, then it might not be all that lucrative. There may be a scenario of too much supply resulting into lower prices; to attract more sales and to create more room for addition of new stock.

Note: Quail products intended for sale in supermarkets should be neatly packed and clearly labeled. Doing so will help you acquire more sales and sales leads, and may expose a quail farmer to more sales opportunities.

Reach Out to Food Nutritionists

Due to quail's meat being a favorite alternative source of white meat, the demand for the meat plus quail eggs has continued to register an increase in demand from an increasing number of food nutritionists. Your task is therefore, to compile an up-to-date list of nutritionists in your region, and inquire from them if they could be in need of any quail product.

One beautiful thing about working with nutritionists is that they are usually attached or linked to certain organizations or institutions. If successful, you may end up getting links to such institutions, and subsequently have more kill.

Target Specific Individual Households

Due to the continued recommendation of white meat over red meat by health experts, most nutrition savvy households are best positioned as reliable customers for quail products.

There are many families, world over, where a breakfast without an egg is regarded as no breakfast. If there are such families nearby, and even others who may be frequent or even infrequent consumers of quail products, then try reaching out to them. Stay alert and establish as many contacts as you possibly can.

Target Hospitals, Other Government & Private Institutions

As an alternative source of white meat and protein, most hospitals readily recommend to their ailing patients the consumption of quail meat over the common red meat. Any serious quail farmer should find avenues of partnering with such nutrition savvy hospitals in order to make available quail products, should they be in need of any.

Equally, a number of government institutions are usually in demand for quail products to be consumed during breakfasts, lunch breaks, or when they congregate for meetings / conferences. Any deal or contract secured by a farmer to supply quail products to such government or private institutions is usually rewarding.

Target Local Markets

Start selling quail products in local markets, especially in those areas/local markets around where you stay. It is often said that good things are usually nurtured at home. Then slowly, expand to other markets within the same region. And finally you can target other markets in within your country, and then across the globe. Dream big, start small and work on your progress.

Target Local and International Non-Governmental Organizations

There are several local and international non-governmental organizations working in drought prone areas. Equally, there are other Ngo's whose missions are nutrition based. These and other similar Ngo's are usually good targets to sell quail products to. Get in touch with such organizations.

Target Agricultural Exhibitions

Try to find a space or stand whenever there are local agricultural exhibitions i.e. during local agricultural shows, agricultural related exhibitions, or any other forum or event that might attract the interest of consumers of quail products.

Being present in such events will help you build more useful contacts and help you generate more sales and sales leads. Many successful quail farmers have benefitted a lot from being present in such similar exhibitions. Do not be left behind.

Give Free Samples

Whenever your neighbors, friends and relatives pay you a visit, give them a few samples of products from your quail farm. Next time, some of these people may turn into your lifetime supporters (in form of clients).

There is a golden sales rule *that people often would buy first from people they know or trust.* What you are doing by giving out free samples is building on that trust with potential clients. And the end result will be to gain the trust and favorability of these clients. Should they be in need of quail related products, you will be the first person they would want to contact.

Target Various Learning Institutions

There are growing numbers of persons who have become millionaires in the quail farming venture. Notably, due to the continued more positive economic impact of quail farming across the globe, several institutions of learning have continued to be in demand for a variety of quail birds, plus quail products for: breeding purposes, learning purposes, and for consumption. Look out for such institutions and tap into their demand stream.

Be An Effective Ambassador of Your Brand

Give out your quail farming testimony to your friends and relatives. Equally, willingly mentor or guide other upcoming quail farmers, or persons interested in quail farming. You never know when the gods of good luck might pay you a visit and reward your efforts.

Write emails, text your friends, create a website, develop a catchy and convincing sales pitch to help you eliminate possible sales resistance and to give you an edge over other quail farmers. Aim to make your brand visible within your region. Look out for occasions like church functions, networking forums, group meetings or any other relevant event which might attract the attendance of consumers of quail products.

Woo Customers From Your Competition

We live in an era where customers are in unending pursuit of quality products and services from reliable and credible persons and institutions. Use freebies to lure consumers from your competition, and find ways of retaining them for a longer duration, should they cross over.

Know what the competition is offering and try to outsmart their offer. Equally, generate as many positive feedbacks from your satisfied clients as you can, and use those positive reviews to attract and retain new consumers from your competition.

Keep And Reward Your Current Customers And Find Avenues of Making Them Remain Loyal For Life

Be creative and think outside the box. Find attractive ways of recruiting new customers whilst at the same time retaining the existing ones. A success of any business venture is hinged on loyalty of its clients. If you must reward your clients in order to maintain their loyalty, then never hesitate doing so. But reward them calculatively, so that you do not run into any debt or even close shop due to avoidable losses.

How To Profitably Save or Invest Proceeds From Your Quail Farm

"It's always never too early or too late to start saving: be it for retirement, for short-term purchases, or savings for an emergency reserve. However, the early you start, the better, and you should strive to save first before spending!"

The most secure path towards financial freedom in old age lies in having an excellent savings or investment plan. Upon retirement, or when faced with sudden financial emergencies, your savings or investment kitty will be handy to help you boldly navigate through such financial storms.

It's always never too early or too late to start saving: be it for retirement, for short-term purchases, or savings for an emergency reserve. However, the early you start, the better, and you should strive to save first before spending!

Below are some of the ways you can use to profitably save or invest part of, or even all of your profits from quail farming.

Note: Some of the savings and investments options suggested herein may seem passed by time, but at the end of the day, it all boils down to settling on the ones you feel most comfortable with. *'One man's meat may be poisonous to another man'*. Equally, I have opted to combine both savings and investment options together, even though in theory, the two have different meanings. I've purposely done that for the benefit of the reader.

- **Plough the profits back into the business**

When you feel satisfied with the returns from your quail farm, you can opt to plough back all, or part of your profits into the agribusiness. By doing so, you will have an opportunity to expand on your production, leading to increased yield. Equally, you can opt to start up another quail farm for the same purpose of increasing your production capacity.

- **Invest in a startup business**

Here is how this works. An individual first identifies a new business enterprise with expected good returns. After careful analysis and understanding of the business, she/he may opt to invest in it as an Angel Investor. Once the business breaks even or rakes in agreed returns, then the Angel Investor may either be paid back the original amount he/she invested, plus any other accrued/agreed profits. Equally, the investor may settle on increasing his/her shares or investments.

Any choice the investor has to make depends on the profit margins or returns from such businesses. As an Angel investor, before you decide on investing in any startup business, ensure that you do a lot of background checks. Always choose to make your investments within the existing legal provisions, and stay timely updated on events affecting that business. If possible, aim to invest in businesses in which you have some knowledge on how they operate.

- **Invest in unit trusts**

This is another favorable profitable option offered by several investment banks and insurance companies. Here, your money is pulled together with others' (in what is called a pool), and is thereafter carefully invested by the financial/insurance institution.

The best part of investing in unit trusts is that your money is guaranteed (secure). Your money is totally safe. It is the investment banks or insurance companies who bear the risk associated with investing your money.

If you love to own shares in the stock market, but lack the necessary know-how, then you can start out with investing in unit trusts.

- Join a savings club

A savings club may be another good way to save your proceeds. Notably, a good number of today's respectable investment groups across the globe started off as small savings clubs. For any savings club to thrive, its members must have a clear focus on where they intend to be in future, and religiously commit to achieving their club's set objectives.

The most common model for most savings clubs entails members contributing a specific or agreeable amount(s) of money at designated times, spread throughout the year. Upon meeting specific goals, members may then decide to either invest, or divide the accumulated or contributed money.

- Open a savings account

This is one of the most secure options for saving any amount of money. I would highly recommend that you open a savings account if you intend to save some cash towards a particular project, or just to attain a specific desired financial goal.

Notably, most financial institutions would levy certain charges from your savings account at the point of withdrawing the money, or when you opt to withdraw your money before the stipulated time (before allowable withdrawal periods). You should therefore understand the terms and conditions of the savings account you intend to operate before you commit to opening it.

- **Open a fixed deposit account**

This is another exciting option offered by financial institutions. They allow you to deposit or invest a specific amount of money for a given period of time, at an agreed interest rate.

Using a fixed deposit account may be better than merely opening a savings account, since it has better returns on investment. However, you will be required to deposit your money for a specific period of time, without withdrawing any portion of it. In return, your money will yield some interest, payable at the end of the agreed period.

- **Invest in government bonds**

This is another risk-free and profitable way to save your money. Most bonds offered by various governments to investors, local or international, work in a similar way as the fixed deposit accounts. They have a fixed interest rate which you are made aware of before investing your money. You therefore, have an opportunity to calculate the expected returns and thus, make a meaningful decision before committing your money.

- Invest in the stock market

This option is best suitable for economic savvy persons: those who can correctly forecast future performances of companies listed in stock markets. However, with some good advice from trustworthy stockbrokers or investment advisers, you can take a stab at this option.

There is an old aged connotation that *'we loose 100% of chances we do not take.'* Truth is, most people tend to shy away from investing in the stock markets. This fear has give room to a smaller portion of the population who are currently reaping heavy returns from various stock markets across the globe. You can start small, and grow your confidence with time.

- Shylocking

Let me start off with a disclaimer from its definition. According to *freedictionary.com*, shylocking is defined as *lending money at exorbitant interest rates*. Shylocking is an age-old practice of lending money by an individual to other individuals, formally or informally. Engaging in shy locking isn't for the faint at heart. It's for the brave risk takers! You may have borrowed some cash one time from a friend, colleague, or relative. If the person opted to charge you some interest out of that borrowed cash, then that act is what is regarded as shylocking.

World over, many governments regard shylocking as a form of money laundering, since many people have ended up accumulating massive wealth which they can't rightly account for, out of proceeds from the sometimes high interest rates that this practice attracts.

In shy locking, it is the responsibility of the lender to decide whether to charge or not to charge interest on the amount he/she is giving out. This approach poses a legal challenge to the lender should the borrower fail to pay back. It is therefore, a risky and unpopular way of saving or investing any money. However, it can work best if there is some mutual trust between the borrower and the lender.

The Five Most Common Quail Farming Mistakes You Should Avoid

"Truth is, quail farming is a lucrative venture. However, it's only lucrative to a farmer who is not only patient, but is equally willing to go the extra mile and have in place all quail raising requisites"

First Mistake
Rush to make a quick kill

Who doesn't love getting some quick money? I guess not so many people. However, this is one area which has killed dreams of the many would be successful quail farmers. It is true that too much ambition can kill a man!

Truth is, quail farming is a lucrative venture. However, it's only lucrative to a farmer who is not only patient, but is equally willing to go the extra mile and have in place all quail raising requisites.

Any farmer whose focus is fixed on making quick returns out of this venture, without the necessary inputs is bound to be miserably frustrated, and must eventually fail!

Second Mistake
Purchasing of already egg-laying birds for purposes of commercial egg production

When quail begin laying eggs, it is never easy for an inexperienced quail farmer to tell their exact ages. It is therefore possible for such a farmer to purchase quails in their third year of egg-laying, or quails approaching egg-laying-menopause (if the purchase is made at the egg-laying stage).

It is interesting to note that in terms of growth, quail do slow down and would eventually stop putting on more weight as their approach full maturity. Therefore, just by looking at the size of any quail bird, at times, it would not be easy to tell its exact age.

It is equally proven through research that female quail do lay eggs consistently within their first years of egg production. However, in the subsequent years, their rate of egg production may slow down, or may become inconsistent, and eventually disappear as they age. Did you know an egg laid by a four-year-old quail may be infertile? This would therefore result into massive waste of resources and time by any farmer on such birds, especially if the farmer intends to incubate produced eggs.

It is recommended that for commercial quail farming, especially for egg production, a farmer should aim to purchase utmost, five weeks old quail birds. At that stage, their vitality and productiveness is guaranteed. However, if a farmer has the capacity to hatch quail eggs then that would be the most recommended option.

Third Mistake
Starting Quail farming without relevant approvals or permits

Did you know at one point in history, quails almost became extinct? Therefore, in order to preserve and increase their numbers today and in future, most governments world over do classify quail as endangered wild birds. They then provide for their protection through certain legislations.

If you reside in a country where such legislations do exist then you need to do the right thing: get relevant approvals before venturing into rearing the birds. You can never play hide and seek with the authorities forever. There is a common that '*the Government has long arms*'. If you therefore decide to keep quail without relevant approvals, then it would possibly not take too long before relevant authorities catches up with you.

Fourth Mistake
Worrying about where to sell quail products even before starting quail farming

Worrying about where to sell quail products is a common habit amongst many people who want to venture into quail farming. But then, let's be realistic here. Why would you be worried of the existence or non-existence of markets to products you do not even posses in the first place? It beats any viable logic.

Generally, a number of successful and sustainable business enterprises are mostly driven by passion, and not any anticipated huge returns. When you have passion in what you do, then the proverbial *the rest will fall in their respective places* will eventually follow. Finding a lucrative market for your quail products would not take long before realizing once you rightfully start off the venture.

Fifth Mistake
Starting quail farming without a clear plan on what one intends to achieve

It is usually advisable to start any serious business venture with a business a plan. However, in quail farming, one does not necessarily need one, but must plan to incorporate it along the way for long term benefits.

What do you really want to achieve out of your quail farming venture? An anonymous best put it that *failing to plan is a perfect plan for failing*. Lack of proper planning usually leads to several desperate acts which may eventually push any quail farmer to start focusing on short term returns rather than on the long term returns.

A typical example of lack of planning and loss of focus would be to start quail farming with say, over a thousand birds, only to sell almost all the birds at throw-away prices. Then at some point again, be tempted to start rearing the birds again. If such might be your focus then stock market trading best suits you. However, even in the stock market, the whole environment is usually unpredictable and demands for patience and consistency.

Frequently Asked Questions About Quail Farming

"Must I first get approval before keeping quail? **What are some of the general requirements for keeping quail?** *Where can I get quail chicks and fertilized eggs?* **How much does a quail chick go for? Are quail birds affected by weather?** *Where can I sell products from my quail farm?* **At what age should I get quail chicks for purposes of breeding?"**

Must I first get approval before keeping quail?

In certain countries, it's considered unlawful to raise quail without certain approvals from relevant government departments. This they do mainly to protect the birds from extinction. Yes, you may need a License/Permit/Approval before you start rearing quail. (But this rule differs from one country to another. There are certain countries where you may not need any permit to raise quail).

Find out from your country's Wildlife/Agricultural or any other relevant government institution charged with the responsibility of issuing the approvals on what is required of you before you begin raising quail.

What are some of the general requirements for keeping quail?

In a number of countries where permits are prerequisites to keeping quail and other select birds and poultry breeds, you may be required to first build an appropriate house (cage) for the birds. Equally, you must put in place other relevant infrastructure necessary for raising the birds. You'll then provide details of your location (the place where you intend to raise the birds), and finally, you may be required to pay certain charges or fees. It's that simple!

Where can I get quail chicks and fertilized eggs?

Always remember that if you start with undesirable breed, you'll end with undesirable output! The type of quail breed you are raising usually determines the quality of gains you will extract from them. One convenient way of getting quality quail breed, or quality fertilized eggs for hatching is by first getting a firsthand experience on how a quail farm is run (if it's your first time). Therefore, visit at least three different quail farms within your area or region to get that firsthand experience. Thereafter, you can get your initial flock from established breeders located within your area. You can liaise with established quail farmers in your region to get an updated list of recommended quail breeders in your region.

How much does a quail chick go for?

The current prices for quail chicks and other quail products do vary from one farmer to another and from one region to another. World over, quail farmers are currently enjoying an open-priced-market; where each and every farmer has the ability to determine the price of his or her quail products.

Therefore, there isn't any standard price pegged on quail chicks. However, several countries have reported the selling of the chicks at prices ranging between $2 to $10, depending on the age, breed, and location of the quail farmer/breeder.

Are quail birds affected by weather?

Quails are naturally hardy birds, but yes, they are affected by extreme temperatures (too hot or too cold temperatures). Under such conditions, closely monitor the birds and when necessary, provide for them some cooling or heating sources, respectively.

Where can I sell products from my quail farm?

First, you need to read the section on this book on *Simple Strategies For Marketing And Selling Quail Products*. But all in all, you can sell your quail products to fellow farmers (those looking for breeding chicks, fertilized eggs etc). Equally, you can package the products and supply to local supermarkets, hypermarkets, and food stores. You can also sell the products at the local market. And last but not least, you can liaise with the local hotels and restaurants and seek to supply them with the products (meat and eggs).

At what age should I get quail chicks for purposes of breeding?

From personal experience, the best age to get quail chicks for purposes of breeding is at one week old. However, at that stage, they are usually fragile and demand a lot of care and attention. Quail chicks beyond one week old are sometimes slightly expensive and in most cases, an average quail farmer may never tell their exact ages and sexes.

Other Related Books

- **BEST QUAIL BREEDS**: 10 types of quail breeds that are good layers and are best to keep for their meat

- **QUAIL FARMING FOR BEGINNERS**: A quick A to Z beginners' guide on raising healthy quails

- **QUAIL DISEASES**: Identification and management of stress, vices, and diseases in quails.

- **QUAILS 101**: The most asked questions and answers on quail farming

- **QUAILS**: About Raising Quails

Made in the USA
Monee, IL
17 September 2021